PETS

Jokes

Wacky words compiled by Greg Lee
Daffy drawings made by Robert Court

The Rourke Corporation, Inc.
Vero Beach, Florida 32964

Lee, Greg, 1956-
    Pets / Wacky words compiled by Greg Lee.
       p. cm. — (The little jokester)
    Summary: Jokes and riddles about pets. Example: What happens if your dog swallows a watch? It gets ticks.
    ISBN 0-86593-266-2
    1. Pets—Juvenile humor. 2. Riddles, Juvenile. [1. Pets—Wit and humor. 2. Jokes. 3. Riddles.] I. Title.
II. Series: Lee, Greg. Little jokester.
PN6231.P42L44 1993
818'.5402—dc20
                                       92-43964
                                          CIP
                                           AC

Produced by The Creative Spark
San Clemente, CA.

Where does a sheep get its haircut?
At a baa-baa shop.

What do you get when you cross a monster with a cat?
A neighborhood with no dogs.

Why do dogs growl?
Because they don't know any dirty words.

Did you hear about the scientist who crossed a rabbit with a skunk?
The rabbit gave him a dirty look.

What did the mouse say to the cat?
"Sorry, but I can't stay for dinner."

What do you get when you cross a parrot with a shark?
An animal that can talk your ear off.

What has two pink ears and writes?
A ballpoint bunny.

How many hairs are in a rabbit's tail?
None, because they are all on the outside.

Policewoman: "Your dog has been chasing the paper boy on a bicycle."
Dog owner: "That's baloney. My dog can't ride a bicycle."

What do you get when you cross a dog with a duck?
A duckshund.

What kind of snake is good at math?
An adder.

Nicole: "My dog has a fever."
Jean: "What did you do about it?"
Nicole: "I rubbed him with mustard."
Jean: "Mustard? Why?"
Nicole: "I always put mustard on my hot dog."

What do you call a 300-pound cat?
Sir.

Customer: "Are you sure this dog is loyal?"
Pet Store Salesman: "Sure. I've sold him five times this week."

Customer: "This birdseed doesn't work. I want a refund."
Pet Store Owner: "What's wrong with it?"
Customer: "I planted some of this last week and not one bird sprouted."

Why are some goldfish not in schools?
They like to play hookey.

What is the difference between a piano and a fish?
You can't tune a fish.

What did the rooster say to the hen?
You must have been a beautiful egg.

Meg: "I took my rabbit to the barber."
Rich: "You're kidding? What for?"
Meg: "To get a harecut."

What do you get when you cross a dog with a toad?
A croaker spaniel.

Why should you never have a kangaroo for a pet?
Because they get hopping mad.

Betty: "Your parakeet is really quiet today. I thought it talked."
Joe: "It does, but we're not speaking to each other."

Is it possible for a dog to have a favorite car?
Sure, if it's a Hounda.

What do cats like on their hot dogs?
Mousetard.

What do you call a rabbit who has fleas?
Bugs Bunny.

Danny: "I see your dog is back from obedience school."
Davey: "Yes, he finished two days ahead of schedule."
Danny: "Pretty smart, huh?"
Davey: "Not really. He was expelled."

What do cats have for breakfast?
Mice Krispies.

Terry: "I've lost my dog."

Malcolm: "Really? Why don't you put a lost and found ad
in the newspaper?"

Terry: "Now there's a dumb idea. My dog can't read!"

Jennifer: "How did your dog get such a flat nose?"

Adrian: "He likes to chase parked cars."

Gary: "What did the veterinarian give your sick rabbit?"
Sherry: "Hare tonic."
Gary: "And your pig?"
Sherry: "Some oinkment."

Why are there so few psychiatrists for dogs?
Because they're always saying, "Get off the couch!"

Did you hear about the 300-pound parrot?
It says "Polly wants a cracker—NOW!"

What happens when your dog travels in an airplane?
It gets jet wag.

Larry: "What kind of dog is that?"
Belle: "A Chihuahua."
Larry: "Bless you."

What do you get when you cross a dog with a cat?
A pet that chases itself.

Mary: "My cat Ralph ate my goldfish."
Beverly: "Did you punish him?"
Mary: "No, but he did get findigestion."

Ashleigh: "I'm going to wash my dog today."
Kyle: "Does she like it?"
Ashleigh: "Yes, she's a shampoodle."

Why didn't Jennifer get a kitten for her baby brother?
Because no one would trade with her.

WITH FUR   WITHOUT FUR

Why do cats have fur?
If they didn't, they would look pretty silly.

      Casey: "It sure is hot today."
      Rob: "Yeah, I just saw my dog chasing a cat, and they
           were both walking."

Which dogs make the best ambassadors?
Diplomutts.

What is the highest honor a cat can receive?
An Acatamy Award.

Policeman: "Hey you got a license for that dog?"
"No, officer. He's not old enough to drive."

What do you call a cat that has lost one of its nine lives?
An octopus.